Love Yourself

A Book For Young Men

By

Joseph Newcombe

About

This book was written to remind young men that relationships are the most important thing in life. This sounds counterintuitive towards the title of the book, *Love Yourself*, but it's not, because loving yourself is a relationship with yourself. It is also the most important relationship you can have. This book offers tips, stories, and thought-provoking ideas through interpersonal and real-life truths of young men in today's world.

Note

This book is non-fiction in nature but some characters, settings, and scenarios have been changed and metaphors added.

Contributions

I sit here isolated during the 2020 COVID-19 pandemic wondering how almost five years have gone by since I wrote this book in University. I realise that this book is meant to be shared with others and it is in times like these that we need to learn to continue to love ourselves. Thank you God, family, friends, and Steven Gooden.

Table of Contents

Preface

Throughout my travels and studies, I have made mistakes, learned, observed, and grown. I hope the lessons I have learned can help inspire you to live a happier life full of joy. Rather than waste my whole life searching for the perfect woman or right career, I want to fill my life with more purposeful pursuits and am willing to sacrifice it all. I have seen the dark side of the world. It is fun for a short period, but it does not last. Soon that fun turns into darkness. I don't want to live in the dark. I want to live an honest life — a life filled with pure zealous passions and experiences. I am tired of wasting my time on false hopes. I know many men who live meaningless lives. They live to fuck and make lots of money. How can you blame them? We are all animals, right?

Our culture is so fixated on what others are doing. We have nowhere to turn to. No inspiration. We are always comparing ourselves to others. We are fixed on what others are doing and thinking, and we neglect ourselves. *We neglect our own talent and gifts by worrying about others' lives.* We lower ourselves to our own minimum. We spend more time on Instagram and

Facebook analyzing other people's lives.

During the process of writing this book, I have dedicated my time to read many books; many of which I never finished. I got lazy and bored. I never fully appreciated the books I read. One thing I have learned about reading and in life, is that you cannot take shortcuts. If you do, you will never fully understand the story, nor will you fully grasp the entirety of the message and its purpose. I encourage you to push yourself to the limits of what you think is possible.

The Set-Up

In a world filled with genocide, school shootings, cheating wives and husbands, thief's, corporate slavery, global warming, terrorism, labor exploitation, racism, addiction, over consumption, lust, and so on—there seems to be a never-ending polluted world. A world where people exemplify behaviors that are not soundly normal. For example, some people think Hitler was a cool guy and often make jokes about the Holocaust at school. This is a world where people use ethnicity to label good and bad. It is so sad to see false hopes in this world because this world is filled with beauty.

I want people to feel loved. I want people to know that there is hope and that there are outlets for the passions that you possess. We let excuses and fear get in our way too often. A lot of people will disagree with my beliefs and perspectives. That is okay. You are entitled to your own opinion. That is what makes you beautiful. However, don't just throw it all away. Use your brain. Think for yourselves and step out of your comfort zone. Do not let fear dictate your life. Do not let the fear of falling keep you from flying.

What is so cool about living in darkness? Where are your borders? How far do you want to push yourself into darkness? We, as humans, are longing for truth. We go our entire life wondering, some of us wonder more, but in general, we are never sure what the future holds. It is scary. Albert Einstein puts it like this,

"A person experiences life as something separated from the rest- a kind of delusion of consciousness. Our task must be to free ourselves from this self-imposed prison, and though compassion, to find the reality of Oneness."

When my father told me who the most important person in this world was, I was confused. He said, "The most important person in this world is yourself." I never fully understood this concept until I hurt someone I loved: myself. My soul hardened and, in turn, I could not love anyone else. It was a selfish point in my life. Loving yourself makes the world a better place because you can love others. We always want what we can't have but usually, it's not what is best for us. Yet, we always want more. This book is a vessel designed to help you realize you are the most important person in the world and that you don't need more. Instead, what you need is to love *yourself.*

Loving yourself is hard. If it was easier

more people would. Loving yourself is ultimately a sacrifice. If you love yourself, you take care of yourself and do what is best for you. Doing what is best for you gives you peace. Some may wonder what is best for me or how do I know what is best for me? I believe only you can answer that question and hopefully, the following chapter can give you inspiration.

Take Off

I walked down the isle of the plane and sat down at seat 24C. Shortly after I sat down, an old stylish man comes flying in with a pink Italian designer shirt with his collar popped up and a shiny gold watch on his left wrist. He sat closest to me in the middle even though his seat was on the outside row. There were three seats in the row, and only two of us! His name was Haimo. He was 80 years old. He was young and sporty at heart. He was assertive. He immediately smiled when he saw me. I knew he was a cool guy.

Haimo had just gotten back from the Canary Islands and was headed to see his son in Munich for the weekend. I would guess he was 60. Haimo and I chit-chat, we make small talk while we wait for the plane to take off, but all of a sudden, he says something out of the blue. One of the first things he says to me in a soft voice in Swedish was, "I have been sleeping with the younger women from all over the world." By young, he probably meant 60-75 years old; I guess you must put it into perspective. He said, "I cannot get enough of it. They love me. I go in and I show them some tango dance and the women love it. It is too easy. I have fun."

Haimo told me about his life. I could see

in his face that he was grateful that I was so interested in him. I admired him. He was 80 years old living his dream of dancing in different countries across the globe and sleeping with women. In my mind, I was impressed; I could not believe he is 80! I thought I could see myself in him, but I realized something—he looked very lonely. Although he had money, time, and energy, he did not seem complete to me. I asked him about his childhood and life story. He offered me some of his beer. We spoke a lot, all in Swedish. It was sometimes hard to understand everything he said because of his thick German accent. However, if I did not understand something, I could see it in his eyes. Throughout our conversation, people kept looking at us. Actually, they were staring at us, as if I was his son. Most of the people on the plane spoke German, so they did not understand our conversation in Swedish. He had been born in 1935, in East Berlin. Leaving his family behind, he escaped East Berlin in his teenage years during the Cold War by riding his bike across the border to West Berlin. He managed to get across unseen by authorities by hiding and sleeping in the bushes. He spent a few nights sleeping in the forest. I was so impressed. I had never met anyone like this ever before. I was inspired. In the 70's, he immigrated to Sweden and started his own business within the coal and mining industry. By then, I guess he had already had two wives and a few kids behind him. He told me about this third ex-wife. She was a Swede, and they did not have any children, but I could see how much he was angry with her. His ex-wife called him when we landed. He yelled at her, "Why the fuck would you call me, you know I am flying." You have wasted my time, you dumb bitch." He did not even give her the chance to talk.

We waited to get off the plane because our gate number had changed, and so I remained in my small airplane seat in an inebriated state of mind, a mental disillusionment. I felt extremely confused because he seemed so empty inside, yet so joyful and nice to be around on the outside. He did not love himself. I could sense that. Even at 80 years old, traveling the world, sleeping around, dancing, and drinking on the beautiful rare exotic beach of this earthly realm, he was lonely.

As I sat there in my seat, I looked forward to my headrest and saw the safety flight information. It showed an illustration of all the exit doors on the plane in case of an emergency. I thought to myself, "How many times do they actually ever use these exits? The more I looked at the front of my seat, the more I began to think about my exit strategy. What's my exit strategy? How will

I survive the crash if all goes wrong?

I asked myself one question, "Joe, if you could be doing anything in the world right now, what would it be?" I answered myself, "I would want to be shooting a short film as the lead actor expressing how I feel about the world and myself. Not like a movie, but a short YouTube movie. That's all I want in the entire world." I then said, "God, if you are real or are even anything close to being real, give me a short movie! That is all I want, to show the world how I feel on the inside because it seems like no one ever understands."

The Black Jesus

I arrived in Los Angeles, California, away from Europe and my normal routines — fresh off the plane. I put my black bomber jacket on as I stepped out of the car. I pulled back my hair with right hand and gently slid my fingers through my hair, pulling the hair out of my face. I grabbed my stuff from the backseat of my car — just a computer, a notepad, and a pencil. Through the motion of pulling my hair back, I could only think of one thing, this is the lowest point in my life. I could not stop thinking about her and all that I had done wrong. I just could not get her out of my head.

The only thing I knew would help get her out of my mind was to distract myself. It does not matter what distraction, but anything to get her out. Yet, ironically, I still want to keep her in mind, she is all I want to think about. I know I need to let go because it is ruining my health. I feel 4 years old. I feel like a child who does not get what he wants from the candy store, even when the child is crying and pleading to get the candy; the tough mom holds firm and does not give into her child's cry.

While driving to the coffee shop from my house, I could barely focus. This is ruining my health. It is tearing me apart. *The pain of not having her, but still having her on my mind.* I need to distract my brain somehow, maybe some beers? Shit, am I still standing here in the parking lot? I need to go in and get a coffee. That is what I came here for in the first place. My mind is all over the place, shit. This is a prison. No escape. Trapped in my own mind of thought. It sucks. There is no way out. Nothing can help me get away from my guilt.

I wish I knew a way; I wish could erase all my memories and start over. As I took the first step forward towards the coffee shop, I anticipated meeting someone new. I had a gut feeling, a feeling that this person would be able to get rid of my thoughts of her. I don't know why I had this sensation of anticipation. Do you know that gut feeling? When you are not 100% sure that something is going to happen, but more like 70% sure something is going to happen. Yeah, that is me. I was hit in the gut with this feeling. The thought of a single women waiting for me inside of Starbucks pondered in my thoughts; a woman looking for a man to come sweep her off her feet. What the fuck was I thinking? I could barely stand on my own two feet. I opened the door at Starbucks.

The first person to make eye contact with me was a 5' 11" black man wearing orange and blue running sneakers, a black suit, and a red flannel. He had slim black shades on his forehead. They looked like speed dealer sunglasses. He came close to me as I headed towards the counter to order my drink. He patted me on the shoulder and smiled proudly. He said to me in a confident voice, "How did church go?" It was one of the weirdest encounters I have had with anyone before. Why did this guy's words upset me so much? I do not go to church. I don't believe in God. Why would he say a thing like that to me? He does not even know me. He must be a crazy ass drug dealer. Ah, what do I care? I have weird random people talking to me all the time. But this encounter was different than the rest. I felt free. My blood and heart starting racing like a racehorse. At that point, I was feeling even more emotional than before coming to Starbucks. When he touched my shoulder, it was if he sent an electric shock down my spine.

Wow! I had not thought of her a few minutes! I got her off my mind! I felt relieved. For a short period of time, I managed to distract myself. I heard someone over my shoulder, "Joe, Joe, your coffee is ready." Whoops! I had forgotten about my coffee. I made my way to the outside patio and sat at the nearest table to the door. I flipped open my laptop and slightly slipped the dangerously hot coffee. The sun beamed into my eyes, it felt amazing.

Black Jesus meets me

This is Black Jesus's interpretation of meeting me:

There I sat consumed with grief and purpose. My nephew just days earlier was shot dead. My family was in mourning 3,000 miles away. Why was I sitting here in this loneliness? I told myself I needed to go out, to sit amongst humans, perhaps I'd meet someone who'll distract me long enough to feel like my normal self.

Maybe a stranger will need what I can offer, and I'll rescue them and satisfy my need to feel needed, wanted, and free of self-grief. They could dissuade me from my spiraling self-pity and fear of traveling to a grieving family, most of whom I've not seen in 20 years. I went get a coffee, but I once I arrived, I immediately wanted to turn around, but I pressed on. I ordered a black coffee and cinnamon swirl cake. I surveyed the room, but everyone is engaged in conversation with others, if not intimately so with their technology whores, lol. I sat alone praying someone would sit next to me or that a new patron would walk in and catch my eye. None do. And now I have decided to abandon this idea and crawl away.

As I prepared to leave, my spine tingled and my heart beat faster. I felt an unusual rush and my spider-like senses went crazy. When I looked at the street outside, I saw an unearthly surreal man walking towards me. He was so strange and unusual, that I began to scan the room to see if anyone saw or noticed the figure walking in, but oddly none do. I knew in that instant, that he was there for me. I felt him before he even opened the door. I saw three of him. An artist, a businessman, and a worldly man.

When he entered, I saw a light and a strength, but I also saw a hunger too, as if he's searching or looking for something.

He had the face of a God, wait no, a face of a pure angel. I saw his purity, his love, and his heart. I was compelled more than I was drawn. I must touch this man. I walked out, wishing I could have stayed to talk with him, but I had to go. When I passed him, I touched his shoulder and said to him, "How was Church?" He looked in my eyes and I felt his soul. I knew him at that moment. I walked out but was now consumed with him, obsessed with him. I began questioning myself. Why did I, of all people, not stay with him? I usually do, but this time I didn't.

Ten, maybe fifteen minutes pass and I knew I had to go back find him. I prayed he did not leave. As I turned the corner, he was there, sitting alone and somewhat focused. I approached and re-introduced myself, hoping he did not reject me. I had little time, so I had to be direct. He seemed to expect me. I asked him if I could have lunch with him tomorrow. He agreed, which surprised me. We exchanged numbers and I walked away. I was stirred, somehow filled with joy and love. God sent him and I knew it.

Conversation with Black Jesus

Suddenly there was the man again, he was racing towards me. I asked myself, "What could this guy possibly want from me?" I was not in the mood to talk, but deep down all I wanted to do is talk. I just wanted someone to help mentor me. I had lost hope. The only thing that could help was a cigarette. It would kill the ache in my brain. It almost felt like lack of sleep. Well, I was very tired. Considering I had been traveling for 40 hours the night before and had been in four different countries. So, I was tired, but I still really wanted a cigarette. I wanted to relax. I felt tense. I wondered what this guy was going to ask me. I had no clue. Does he work for the government? Or is he a manager of some sort trying to solicit to me in some way? What is he selling? What could he be after?

I sat in my chair outside the Starbucks and slowly looked up. He came up to me and opened his mouth. He had pearly white, perfect looking teeth. He looked like a God, a black Jesus of some sort. No, a black Jesus and a drug dealer mixed with a dork in his early 40's. I was so curious, so fascinated by him because I couldn't read this guy. I can usually tell who someone is by looking at them, but not him.

He asked me in a soft confident voice, "What do you do?" Do you write music? Are you a musician? I waited a second before I responded. I crossed my legs, like you would in a business meeting, and held my right palm on top of my brown leather chelsea boot. I half smirked back at him and said, "No, I am student."

He quickly answered back with excitement in his voice, "I study political science and I am an author!" Immediately, I was captivated. I liked to write, and I also studied political science. He explained himself, but I couldn't fully understand what he is saying. His mouth was moving, but I was not taking in the words. It was as if he was in fast motion in my head, like when you fast-forward a movie. You get an idea for what is going on but cannot hear the details. I only heard five distinct words: America, Europe, Jesus, Muslim, and NSA.

At the end of his speech, he assertively said, "I want to do lunch with you tomorrow. Meet me at 11:30 tomorrow." I had nothing to lose and no real plans, so I agree to meet at 11:30 tomorrow. We exchanged numbers and he sent me a link to his book. He then proceeded to leave, he disappeared like a ghost. I had no idea where he went. He just vanished.

Broken

We decided to meet in a front of the pier in Seal Beach at 11:30. I was there at 11:25. I did not see him till 11:35, until I heard my name being yelled behind me. There was Steven, the guy I had met at Starbucks. I had no idea what to think of him. No clue what he was up to. We walked and talked by the beach. Everything moved so fast. My mind was spinning because it was on other things than the present. I was thinking about her, I was thinking about my safety with this guy. I had no clue who he is.

Should I be worried? He is not going to kidnap me, is he? I really was not in the mood to be kidnapped. We talked about American history, we talked about the corruption in our society and corruption within religion, and we also talked about what I wanted to do before I went to college. All these topics really bothered me, but they all interested me. So, I listened. I gave him a chance. Everywhere we walked he seemed to know everybody. I did not get it. It made me trust him though.

We had lunch at this place called Crème, which was up the street on Main Street. As soon as we walked through the door, Steven owned the place. All eyes were on him, even people sitting having conversations turned and looked at him, then me. It was as if he was a celebrity. Some people seemed to enjoy his presence, but there were some people who hated him, you could see it in their eyes. We sat outside on a nice European styled patio. Beatrice, our waitress, handed us our delicious warm food. Then Steven turned to me and he said, "Joseph, you have gifts and you are going to write a book." Little did he know, or so I thought he knew, I had always wanted to write a book. It felt great to hear it from him. Even though it did not mean I was going to write a book.

We sat next to a young couple, a big

football-looking guy with a clean cut black beard and a nice looking lady with dark hair. Steven automatically made a connection with them. Steven talked to the football-looking guy about his past and where he is going in the future with the nice lady beside him. After the conversation, the bearded man, said, "How do you know all this stuff about me?" Then Steven referred him to his book and gave him his contact information. I was impressed with Steven. I thought to myself, "Yah he is good, really good." The lunch at Crème was amazing, by the way. It reminded me of a cafe I once ate at in the south of Spain.

After lunch, we walked back down to the

boardwalk by the beach. He brought up God and we talked about my past. I was really struggling with myself. I was broken. I saw hope in hanging out with Steven. Not like an easy quick fix hope, but I knew something beautiful would come out of being friends with Steven. I spoke calmly, "Steven, I trust you." That's when I died a little inside. He sang a song. It was beautiful, "White as Snow, White as Snow." It put me on the verge of tears because it was so beautiful. After he sang that song, I felt brand new. All my guilt and pain vanished. I did not feel heavy; the weight on my shoulders was gone. I was still extremely broken, but I felt like a new person.

Pay attention now, remember that prayer that I had on the plane two days earlier, well, God had answered my demand. This is when everything changed. Steven pulled out a camera. I asked him, "What is that?" He said, "Joseph, I shoot short films." He wanted to do one with me right there at the beach. He wanted to shoot a film about my life. I really could not believe what was going on. Is this really happening? Is this really the omniscient power answering my prayer? I had only demanded this short film two days ago, and now it was happening by itself. I couldn't believe it!

Lunch from Steven's Perspective

I didn't know what to expect upon our second meeting. I only knew or felt it had to happen, that it was already predestined that I should know this man. I parked at quite a distance, being my love to walk. Plus, I enjoyed Seal Beach and the waves. The day prior, the waves were huge, so I brought my camera hoping to catch some footage as I usually do. As I made my way to the pier where I was to meet Joseph, I was disappointed at the waves, they were smaller today. I snapped a few but as I walked along the boardwalk, I took noticed a Christmas flag flying in the wind from the balcony of a beach house, then a goldfish kite on another perch. Nothing fancy, new, or dramatic. It was actually kind of bland, yet I felt an urge to record it. I decided not to and kept walking, but as I passed by I got an unction in my spirit to turn around and record the kite. Why? I don't know. I just did and continued to the pier to meet Joseph. I was a few minutes late. As I approached, he was so distracted that I had to yell out his name. He turned and waved. I asked him if we could walk and talk, which was my habit.

We walked and talked, both of us nervous and excited, because it appeared so random. I wanted to feel him out before eating lunch with him. Checking him for wax haha. He was so honest, well spoken, confident, and strong. Yet, troubled by something. Also, sad. He looked like a sad angel. His hair was blonde, curly, and on fire with the light of the sun. He was well dressed and well mannered. He was pleasant and interesting to me, more European than Californian, which I preferred. We ate at my favorite cafe, Crème. It was neat observing him observing my interactions with people I knew and with strangers. He got to see me in action, in my element. That way, I wouldn't have to explain to him who I was, he could see it genuinely play out. By the end of the lunch we had more interactions and encounters with all sorts of people, and had shared our own stories with each other. We decided to make a short film, as is my habit. I had my camera and a willing participant. It seemed planned but it wasn't. It was cathartic for Joseph. It was a healing and release, a freeing and letting go. It was a baptism of change, a change that was just beginning...for both of us.

The Philosopher

There I was about to order my delicious glass of Guinness at the bar, when two older looking guys, in their upper 40's, looked at me. They broke the ice and made conversation with me. They said something about a lady. I was not sure what though. Then they said something about the lady again, and one of the guys turned to me and whispered softly, "Check out her ass, I would..." Then he said something about his wife and how she was not here right now, she was in a different county. He then told his friends about the rules of the game. If she was not from the same county, she was fair game. Then he looked me and said, "What she does not know won't hurt her, hahahaha, he chuckled deeply."

I went outside and joined the two other guys with my Austrian friend. The guy I just met at the pub had a PhD in Philosophy; he was a professor at one of the Universities in England. He told the group of four us about his previous three girlfriends. He said he cheated on every single one of them. We had a nice group talk. We looked over the city throughout the night. It was beautiful, all lit up. It was just gorgeous. But the conversation really turned when my

Austrian friend opened up and told us about his situation with his girlfriend. He was on exchange, studying his masters; he really loved his girlfriend that was back in Austria. He told us that the women kept coming up to him in Lisbon and it was becoming a problem because he was becoming tempted. I mean, this guy is a great looking giant Austrian-German looking dude, I get it. But he confessed to the group that he did not want cheat on his girlfriend. He loved her, but sometimes it was just too hard to resist.

The Austrian said, '"I have resisted so many times, all perfect 10's." They won't not leave me alone." The women just throw themselves at me. I was at the beach other day and this girl came up to me and took her top off right in front of me and then bent over 10 ft. in front me. It is just like, why? Why me? I don't want this. I have a girlfriend that I love. He was sad because he really did not want to cheat on her. The other guys laughed at him, while I sat and listened. But the other guys stood there and encouraged him to sleep with all these women. The professor said, "What they do not know, won't hurt them." The Austrian said, "Yeah, I guess you are right." Then went dead silent. Everyone in the group stopped and thought for a moment. Then the philosopher professor said, "Just sleep with them, your girlfriend is in Austria sleeping with other guys, you don't know what she is up to. How can you predict her intentions?"

The Austrian, said, "Yeah, I guess you are right, I don't know what she is doing in Austria. But you know what professor, I love her and my relationship with her means too much to me to break over some stupid one night stand with someone I do not even know. It is not worth it; I would regret it for the rest of my life." All the others still encouraged him to cheat and told him he was not a man for not sleeping with the others. I remember just thinking very deeply, "That is a professor, who is hanging out with us at age 40 something and is still single and unhappy." That's when the professor opened up. He broke down and started crying in front of the entire group in a public place. We walked down the street to a more isolated place, where other people could not hear us. He told us his life story and how he regrets everything. He wished he could take everything he has done back in his life, but he sees no hope. He does not even know what is right or wrong. He has no hope in anything.

The Player

Why did being the player messed up the philosopher? He felt empty every time he slept with someone new. Yeah, sure, the next day he felt nice, but he really felt empty inside. I think this is how Haimo felt, the 80-year-old man I met on the plane. The truth about the game (playing women) is that it works, but it can destroy if you are not careful. He had to learn this the hard way. He ended up hurting the girl of his dreams. He had his real girl when he was 20. At the time, he did not know she was the girl of his dreams, but she was.

For him, being a player is fun. It is a never-ending roller coaster of high and low emotions. It became addicting. Some guys look up to you and some women become more attracted to you for being a player. It is a lifestyle. It takes practice. He did not consider himself a player. He said, "I never intended to hurt a woman. I have always wanted the best for a person." I think most people do. Sleeping around with multiple women is not satisfying in the long term. It is short lasted fun and it is demeaning to yourself. You take a part of yourself out every time you sleep with someone new. Sex is like glue, it sticks emotionally, and the more women you sleep with, the more glue you must carry with you. It kills you. It does not feel good at the end of the day. The next morning feels awesome, you have a rush of testosterone, but then you want more. You want more and more. It will never be enough. Do not fall into the false trap of false hopes.

Even Neil Strauss, the top-selling author of *The Game,* says that the whole point of picking up women is to get out of the game. Yet, for many guys, they find some sort of peace in gaming girls. Neil says in the end of the book,

"We were all searching outside ourselves for our missing pieces, and we were all looking in the

wrong direction. Instead of finding ourselves, we'd lost our sense of self…. A blonde 10 in a two- set at the Standard didn't have all the answers. The answers were to be found within."

Sleeping around with multiple women does not make you satisfied. It leaves you longing and aching for more. I know people who have become infatuated with the sexual being. It takes them to new dimensions. When I talk about dimensions, what I really mean is a new perspective, a new truth. The way people begin to see the world is different. You see things through a different set of eyes and in turn it affects your life. Do not chase women, chase yourself, and the right woman will follow. If you chase women, you will end up wanting more and you will never truly be comfortable with yourself. You will never have a sense of peace in your heart.

Poisoned Lovers

Audrey was a smart girl and a financial accountant. She was a woman with class and style. She was one of those sexy women who could grab the attention of a group of six men and make their heads turn and jaws drop with slobber on their faces. She was also a cheater. She had a boyfriend for two years, but she was cheating on him with another guy named Diego, sober and sometimes high, every day and night for months. Diego was an innocent young man. He did not have much experience with other women. On the other hand, Audrey had more experience with other men. Audrey and Diego both studied on exchange at the University of Amsterdam for one semester. Audrey's boyfriend worked as an investment banker in New Zealand. Audrey had already planned a 4-month trip around Europe with her investment banker boyfriend before she started sleeping with Diego. At first, Diego did not know Audrey was in a committed relationship.

Diego had a choice after he found out Audrey had a girlfriend. But, once he tasted the sweet poison, there was no turning back. The two poisoned lovers had an addictive habit. They loved each other, they loved each other bodies, and they loved the feelings and smells they produced when being with each other. Others may have known what was going on, but no one said anything. Everyone stood on the sidelines and watched the sinful lovers continue their poisonous addiction. It was very hard for Diego because he was also cheating on another girl. Although it was not as serious as Audrey's relationship, it was still harmful for the other girl. Diego had a moral dilemma. Diego was a good man. He had good values. His heart was torn between right and wrong and the sweet, sweet feeling of love. Love can do that to a man. It can tear your heart out and put in new places. Dark places.

It was only one week until Audrey's boyfriend came to Amsterdam to travel around Europe with her and she still had not told her boyfriend about her cheating on him. Diego told me about the last time they slept together. The boyfriend had texted Audrey:

"Hey baby see you soon <3 I'm one hour away from the airport! I will meet you at your place! Love you<3.

It had been three months since they had seen each other. Diego was still at Audrey's apartment when she received this text. She had forgot about the flight and his early arrival. The double-crossed lovers were sprawled flat out over the white bed sheets, which were stained with the aftermath of sex. The sweat and lustful activities. One last time. One last time. The sinful lovers wanted that feeling for just one last time. They managed to sneak in one last session exactly 59 minutes before receiving the text from the boyfriend. Diego told me that the last time he had sex with Audrey was indescribable. It was painful. You could consider it break up sex, times 500. It was different because the boyfriend was now only 30 minutes away from. The energy was crazy. Diego felt happy and excited about what he had done, but as he walked away from her apartment, he realized how fucked up the situation was. He had just passed Audrey's boyfriend walking into the door as he passed out of the hallway from her apartment. He had no idea who he was, but Diego knew everything. He wanted to say goodbye. The thought of never seeing her again dawned on him. He was in pain. How ironic? Upstairs, Audrey quickly changed the bed sheets and scents the room with fresh incense. Within seconds she quickly freshened up and destroyed any trace of sexual activity.

A few weeks passed by and Audrey was still traveling with her boyfriend. She was reluctant to tell her boyfriend about her sinful past. Scared of the pain and loss she would cause by telling him about her poor decision-making, she kept it all in. She could not live with herself. The lie ate her alive, from the inside out. She had to text her ex-lover. The pain of fucking someone else, someone over your true love who you truly care about, at the same time, stabs them in the back and sucks the relationships out of the both of your souls. It is sad. It is un-pure. Relationships are too precious to throw away like this.

KARMA

Karma is a bitch! "What they don't know won't hurt them." It is a common quote and idea that holds fast in society. It is accepted by many to be true. This is a lie. 99% of the people out there think this is true in some respects. I have worked in three different restaurants and in the kitchen it common to use this quote. You might not want to hear this, but I am going to tell you anyway. When the cook drops the piece of salad that was supposed to be on your burger, they will put it on the burger anyway. Heck, the cook's train of thought is "the person eating it will never know." So, why should they waste the lettuce, it just needs a little water and it is fresh as new. What the cook does not know is that that floor is contaminated with meat blood from the other cook's preparation of the burger patties. The cook still uses the cross-contaminated lettuce and hands it the waitress to serve to the table. Why is it that our society has accepted this? Why do we stand for this? Have we not learned that, "Everything that is put out, comes back"? KARMA!

Travel and open your mind

Even though traveling and seeing places can be fun, it is only a short escape from reality. Eventually, when you land or come home from a trip all the same problems and people are there. You should be careful to realize that just because you travel or move halfway across the world does not mean that your life will be any different. On the other hand, sometimes it is just nice to get away and escape reality. I guess that is why people take vacations. To me, it seems sad to have to escape reality because you are not satisfied with reality. It is almost as if people are running or trying to escape themselves.

Traveling does open the opportunity to learn about yourself and other people. Traveling helps eliminate and recreate previous biases and perceptions that you hold. In other words, you allow yourself to open up to new ways of living and thinking, and in turn, you are able to appreciate what you have or don't have. The main point is you can see more and learn more by not staying put in one place. You can spend around the same amount of money as you normally would on just a regular day, not traveling (besides the flight costs). If you plan ahead, it can be very inexpensive.

What I have learned while traveling is that I know nothing about myself. I am seriously so small and tiny compared to anything in this world. Every problem, every thought, every complaint, and every happy moment means nothing to this world besides to a few close friends, family, and yourself. But otherwise this world keeps moving and spinning. The stock market stays open even if you miss your flight. Point is, traveling makes you appreciate "being." The concept of being is taking things as they come and enjoying the moment. This is something that you will learn while traveling. Embrace it!

Throughout your travels you will begin

to learn that the happiest people usually have two things: healthy relationships and a sense of oneness, no matter what race, religion, class, occupation, nationality, they are. Happiness is contingent upon oneself. You control your relationships and you control your state of being. No one else but you. Even in the worst situations you are the only person in control of your state of being. Even in the concentration camps, Dr. Frankl controlled his own mind and survived the Holocaust. Dr. Frankl says,

"Between stimulus and response there is a space. In that space is our power to choose our response. In our response lies our growth and our freedom.

We choose freedom in our own minds, no one else, not even in a concentration camp. Our internal reactions to our external environment are what influence the outcomes of our life.

Offending People for Good

Sometimes we need to hurt others for them to grow. We need to rebuke. I can recall many times when people have scolded me for doing the wrong thing. I have always felt offended by people when they tell me I am wrong. It hurts me. Who are they to tell me that I am wrong? They do not know everything. What gives others the authority to scold someone else? It does not make sense. How can this be?

Most of the time, when someone tells me I am wrong, the other person is usually right. I just don't want to accept that I am wrong. This is a weird concept here; so, let me explain more in detail. I get this feeling in my loin, lower gut feeling that says, "Shit I might be wrong, but what if they are right?" I have two choices here: either I confront this gut feeling and accept it, or I leave it alone and allow myself to think. Generally, my brain, and my intellect that I pull from other people, guides me to go against what the person rebuking me says. It's funny, because although I am wrong and I feel wrong, something keeps me from saying I am wrong. It happens often, and not just to me, but also to a lot of people. When I am driving and another driver does something stupid, I want to confront them and let them know that was stupid. It is hard to do that, but it seems like every time you confront someone like this, they just get madder, and things usually end up worse. This is true. Things to do get worse, people do get hurt, but with time, I have learned that those people that you offend will appreciate it the long run. They might not know it now, but that small comment that you made that night at the New Year's Eve party might have actually saved their lives when they were about to get in the car with a semi-buzzed driver. You might have told your friend how stupid it was to have gotten a ride from your semi-intoxicated friend.

They might have laughed at you and said, dude, he only had 3 beers, stop being such a fucking pussy. But, your friend is wrong. He is wrong because that stupid decision cost him his life. He did not know it then, but if he would have taken your advice four years ago, he would still be eating dinner with his family for Christmas today, but instead he is not. I am not going to go into this anymore, but you get my point: *The smallest things can make the biggest difference. You never know.*

Rainy and Bloody

Here I am sitting in the hospital. I nearly killed him. Steven, aka the black Jesus is a slave. It all happened when we were shooting a short film together. It was one of the craziest moments of my life! Steven's cheek bone popped out of his face. His hair was covered in chocolate. His mouth was full of blood. I knew he is going to be okay, but I did not know the damage that would be done. I felt like an asshole.

Everything just happened so fast. I rushed him as quick as I could to the hospital. He told me, "Joseph, I don't have any medical insurance." In the United States, going to the doctor's costs money, a lot of money, especially if you don't have insurance. Anyways, Steven was wearing a white shirt with mud and stains everywhere. It looks like he had been rolling around in the wet mud, which he had. He was barefoot and wearing half cut blue capri jeans. He was so filthy and wet, it was disgusting. I sat there thankful, so thankful, that I did not kill him, but I almost did. This was one of the funniest and most insane experiences of my life.

I have nearly killed my friend with a shovel! The hardest part about this experience was that we were both still in character. I could not tell at first if he was joking. I was holding the camera and playing my role when I stepped on the head of the shovel. It flipped right up and hit Steven on the side of the cheek, near his temple. Steven was completely out of it. He was hallucinating and going crazy. He was in shock. He does not even know what had happened to him. I could not believe what was going on either. I jumped in the car and drove as fast as I could to the hospital. The hospital would not take us right away. He sat there delusional, he was completely broken. I had never seen him like this. Everyone in the waiting room was looking at us. They had no idea what was going on. All they saw was some white kid dressed in 1800's slave master clothes, with long wide pants and big black boots, and an older black man wearing nothing, barefoot, looking like an 1800's slave. What could they be possibly up to? It must have been surreal for the other patients in the room. Almost funny, but very sad to see the pain in the slave.

I can't even imagine what the others were thinking, especially the doctors. They were probably asking themselves, what the hell just happened?! Well, what had happened was that we created a reality. We created a scene within which I was the slave master and I beat him up, but it all went wrong when he got hacked in the face with a shovel. The shovel nearly killed him. You need to be careful what you wish for, because you might just get it. Steven wanted to recreate what it was like for his black ancestors and he wanted me to play the slave master role because he trusted me. Well, he got it. I almost killed him. He sat waiting in the room still, a cold little slave. When he shivered, the nurse gave him a towel and some socks to warm him a little. I brought him some grape juice from the car and a sweater. We basically replayed Huckleberry Finn, if that is an easier way of understanding what was going on. We sat for about an hour just waiting. We began laughing about how stupid this was and how crazy we were. The blood dripped down his face, but somehow it was funny. We prayed. I remembered we almost got in a car accident on the way to the hospital because it was absolutely pouring. Dr Roca finally took us in the patient room number 2. Steven began messing with the doctors and nurses and was super friendly. He spoke in a British accent. It was so funny, that I could almost not stop laughing, but I knew I needed to because otherwise he just wasting their time and his money.

Then the doctor said something wise that hit both Steven and I. The doctor said, "An injury to your brain is not like an injury to your body." Wow. We instantly thought of relationships, because this was the same as a relationship. That is the whole point in my book, you know? relationships... Sorry, I will carry on with my point. In a relationship, you can hit, or break someone's foot, but if you say something, like break their trust, that goes to the mind. That hit to the mind can never be fixed like the foot, once the damage is there it is hard to get back. The shock of the injury altered Steven's mind. Even though this was serious, we still had fun. While we waited for the results, we ended up shooting an improv film while he laid in the patient bed. Life is too short to dilly-dally, have fun and be serious. Oh...I almost forgot to tell you the beginning of the story, which is the funniest. At first, I dropped him off at the children's hospital. They would not take him. They sent in him across the street barefoot in the pouring rain, and the cops were not very friendly to him.

What Does Love Look Like?

How will you know when you accomplished love? When you are not afraid to offend. When you love, you will not be afraid to hurt the person. True love is not afraid to be offended. The people I am closest to, I am not afraid to offend because I know I am not afraid of losing them. If you feel afraid of losing someone, you are insecure. You see, relationships are all about security. The deepest love is comfortable. Love is when you can sit in the same room with someone and not say anything for hours. You just sit, doing your own thing and minding your own business. You can be comfortable in their presence no matter what the circumstances. Love does not care what others think. Relationships are gold, too precious to carelessly throw away. Relationships are sometimes like marriages, even though they are not marriages. All relationships are based on one core principle: trust. *Trust is the key to relationships.*

In the case of the philosopher, he hurt the person he cared for most when he was younger and never forgave himself for it. He kept on being self-destructive and spread lies to other people to make himself feel better for what he had done. For what? All for nothing. He is ashamed and disgusted of who he has become. Ironically, he is a professor in philosophy, and he is a slave to his own lies. It's funny because as a kid, he never thought he would become this guy. And to think, this person was someone he could have spent the rest of his life with. Someone who made him so happy that the days where no longer days, they were heavenly moments of joy, peace, and happiness. How could he let this happen? How could he live in this fear? How could he live a life like this? He wishes he could go back in time. Not to fix what he did, but to have done the right thing earlier, to confront his mistakes and take responsibility for what he did. The philosopher tried to cover up what he did because he could not dare see her so heartbroken. She meant everything to him. He said, "She was someone every guy deserves, someone that gave more than she took and would go the ends of the earth for someone else." I could see it in his eyes, he felt bad.

Lying is the worst thing anyone can do. Lying does not make things better. Lying destroys you from the inside. It will eat you apart and rot your soul away. The fact that he made some stupid mistake does not bother me as much as the fact that he kept his mistake hidden for so long. He could not handle the truth. It ate him alive.

She relied on him. She thought he was the one. He felt like she felt, that he had all the answers and could solve her problems. In some ways, he did. He brought happiness into her life, but it took a lot of his own energy. He felt like he was getting energy back as well, but there was still something wrong in the relationship that he knew about and she did not.

The philosopher bothered him because he did not know much about it, but he could see that it was weighing her down at the time. Her past relationships always bothered him. Yet, he was too afraid to ever talk about it. He did not want to accept it. He had a hard time, so he kept it all in.

He said something that I will never forget. The philosopher said,

"Am I asking for forgiveness? No. Do I deserve it? No. But what I wish I could do is to let others know that this is not right, and no one should go through this. I wish more young people could learn from others' mistakes because it would be so much easier in their lives."

He said the reason why he cheated was because he feared getting too serious in the relationship, too serious that he would lose himself. He was not satisfied with himself. He said to me, *"You know what is funny, all of this could have been prevented. I have always tried to control my life, but I have been doing it the wrong way."*

The people he hurt and the pain he lives with could have been prevented. It could have been prevented if he had communicated properly. What is so sad, is that the stuff that was holding him down, like goals to coach a rugby team and get his PhD, means nothing to him now. He could have saved the relationship if he had said something earlier. But he did not, and today at age 42 he is still unhappy with himself.

The only thing that matters in life is a relationship. Everything else has no meaning in this world. It really does not. I thought I knew this before, but I did not. I thought I knew relationships were the most important thing. But I did not. I know that with time, pain heals. I just wish there was a right answer, a truth that could set us all free. Honesty is the right thing. Honesty is the truth. The longer you hold your lies in the longer your soul will rot. You cannot change what you have done in the past, but you can change the future of who you are going to be. Honesty is the truth. Communication and people are the only ones that matter in this world. You will not know what love is until you are able to communicate without boundaries, without fear of loss. This is true freedom.

Principles and Values

There are two general things old people say they wish they told their younger selves:

1. Nothing changes, you still feel young when you are old.
2. Stop worrying. ("Don't worry be happy," like that song from Bobby Herring)

Values are universal. They can be seen everywhere. Values are what hold societies together. Without values, we would not have a functioning society. Values come in many different forms. There is no specific value or values that can be defined, because they differ from country to country, city to city, family to family, and group to group. Values are the glue that holds people together.

Principles differ from values. Principles are not universal. They live deep within our core. We are raised with principles. Our parents, or the people that raised us, usually engrave principles into our core when we are young. The core development of principles occurs during the ages of 1-5. Each person has their own principles; they are personal and private. We cannot directly see into someone's principles. They are hidden and deeply embedded into the core of a person. Usually, people cannot even recognize their own principles, but they are there. Principles can be changed.

What is a Man?

What is a man? What principles can guys follow to become a better guy? I know a lot of nice guys that have hurt a lot of women. I do not believe guys are entirely that stupid, as some women tend to think we are. I want to take the time to illustrate what some in society depict a man to be. Then I will illustrate what a real authentic man is in Steven's book, *Always A Groomsman, Never the Groom.*

These are the wrong grooming principles of a man:

- Be Tough = Manly men don't cry =Emotion is a feminine trait
- Fight = Force before diplomacy and reason
- Take It = Be quiet, say nothing, and keep your mouth shut
- Be Athletic = Youth at any cost, focus on sports and body
- Talk Rough = Use threatening, harsh, and hard words
- Be Stylish = Dress like an image - reflect the cultural crowd
- Be a Player = Live like a ladies' man, impress your fellow player
- Pursue Sex = Live by the lust of the flesh

- Play and Party= Be reckless, throw caution to the wind, and ignore consequences
- Make Lots of Money = Cheat, steal, deceive, connive - anything to make more
- Grab Power = Be served rather than serve

These are the right grooming principles of man:

- Be Strong = Face fears reasonably and with courage
- Express Yourself = Release emotions in a healthy way – don't bottle them in or hold them in
- Endure = Bear up under pressure and

don't run away

- Be Healthy = Eat well, exercise moderately, adopt a healthy lifestyle
- Communicate = Words are power -use good vocabulary
- Be Modest =Dress age appropriately and presentably
- Be Honorable = Keep your word, make few vows, and follow through
- Be Moral = Resist temptation, make a weak moment a strong one
- Be Joyful = laugh, smile, play. Life can be hard – take time to have fun
- Be Productive = Work with your hands, do it well, don't be lazy
- Lead = Be humble, serve more than

Love Yourself

you are served, give more than you
take

What is honesty?

The word honesty comes from the word honor. Its meaning is focused on the act of being honorable. In the early 14th century, honesty meant, splendor, honor, elegance, good manners. In the 12th century, from Old French, oneste, honesté, respectability, decency, and honorable action. In Latin, honesty is described as honor received from others' reputation, character, figuratively uprightness, integrity, virtue. Hence, the word honesty is just the act of honor.

I find that a lot of times for me, and

maybe for others, being honest is when you openly share everything. Well it's not. This brings me to my point about honesty: *Some things are better off left unsaid.* This is due to the fact the word honesty, really is an act of being honorable. Being honest does not mean you share everything and tell everything to everyone. I remember when I was a child and there was always that one tattle tale. No one ever liked him because he was not really being honest, he was just trying to make himself look better. It was selfish of him. Was the person being honest? Or was he/she trying to further benefit himself? I remember once, when my teacher asked the students, "Who threw that paper airplane at the back of my head?", the entire class was silent. Everyone looked around at each other, nonverbal communication was at its peak. The whole class looked for verification, a sign on what to do. The teachers said, "The class is not going to recess until someone tells me who threw the paper airplane." The students felt the pressure, the burn of missing the best time of the day, play time, when all the students could go out and be a kid. Some of my favorite memories were from recess. The thought of not being able to go to recess because of one stupid paper airplane irritated me. I always thought to myself, "Relax teacher. Geeez. Take a chill pill."

My point is that honesty is not always about being completely open, it's about being honorable. There may come a time in your life when being honest will be hard to understand and interpret. The best way to know how to handle situations of honesty, is to handle the truth as soon as possible. Take care of what you need to or else other people will get hurt. When the kid who threw the paper airplane did not stand up and take responsibility, the whole class suffered. It was not fair. It was not honorable to not say anything. However, in other circumstances, things are better off kept to yourself, if it is honorable. The "keeping things to yourself" side of honesty is often discussed and debated, but whether it is the best decision comes down to you. The key is to create your own intuition and decide, depending on the circumstance, how things should be dealt with. If you cannot figure that out, ask someone who is close to you who you know will have an objective view, and will not judge or push their opinions strongly on you. The main quality of this person should be one of advisories. By this, the person should look to advise you, not force you to do anything. They should only give suggestions and, of course, this person should be trusted. Overall, *being honest is an act of doing what brings the most honor to someone, something, yourself, and/or all three.*

Taking a Stand

It's like there are two parts of people that say taking a stand is a wrong thing. For some, taking a stand is good, but they worry about the people they might hurt. There is a reason for taking a stand in what you believe in. People should not let anything stand in their way. The philosopher went through a lot of pain and does not want to go back down on the same road again. I guess that is why he finally took a stand and spilled out his life story to us that night.

It is going to be a hard road in front of

you, if you want to take a stand, but it the most meaningful. Making a change is never easy. I wish there was an easy way. You might hope that the people that respect and love you will be there for you when you make the change, but they probably won't. I wish this was a utopia world, where everything is fluffy and perfect. But it is not. There is evil in this world. People are not what you think. People will lie. People will use you to bring you down.

People will lie and use you. Even if you do not see it coming, there are people out there who are looking to drain the life out of you for their own selfish benefit. It happens all the time in friendships, intimate relationships, co-workers, bosses, and so on. Life is too short to dilly-dally. You need to pick and choose who is worth letting in your life. Like a buffet, you choose which food you like to eat. Do not just open your legs and let anyone's cum in. Even if you feel worthless, you can still be repurposed. The same with trash. Trash is recycled, and there is hope. You can be repurposed into something higher and better than its previous use. *It will drain the life out of you if you are not recycled into something better.*

Understanding Yourself

The key to loving yourself is understanding yourself. This exercise will help you understand yourself on a deeper level. It will bring out your true colors that are buried under so many other things in your life. My friend Sam showed me this exercise. He gave me three days to write this. It was one of the hardest things I have ever done.

Having to think about your death, having to face the fact that you will die and most everything you possess on this earth will be meaningless after you die, hurts. This question will take hours to answer, but don't be intimidated, just write. Exclude yourself from any distractions and give yourself at least two hours to sit in peace and silence. Think back to your childhood. What did you enjoy as a kid growing up? What things made you laugh and have fun? What things did you do that brought out the best in you? Here is the formula on how you should answer this question: *First, identify what you want to be remembered for after you die. Second, describe what it means. Third, describe why it is important.* Write down three things that you want to be remembered before you die.

Here is an example of the three things I want to be remembered for before I die:

After I die, I want to be known as a Family Man. Being a family man means being an amazing Father, Husband, Brother, and Son. I want to be known for bringing energy and light into my family's life. I want my family to know that I gave 100%. I want my family to be happy. I want to teach and learn from my kids. I want to learn and grow from my wife. I want to learn to put them first. I want to be known for doing the right thing with my family. I want them to know that I am not perfect, and I make mistakes. I want to be a father who can be open and humble to his family. I do not want to be known as a father who was aggressive and stressed. I do not want to be known as a Father who was not accepting. I want my family to remember how I made them feel. I want my family to know that I am always there for them. I am someone who gave and received love. I know this is important to me because being a family man will give me a sense of purpose and satisfaction.

After you answer this question, you will allow yourself to see who you truly are on the inside. This question is not going to be easy and it may take you days, months, and years to answer. The first time I did this, it took me days. I spent numerous hours working on this question. I still think it took me longer than it should have, but that's okay. Once you identify what you want to be remembered for, you can now reflect on who you are right now to see if it aligns with who you want to be. I remember thinking to myself in my college dorm room, that if this is what I want to be remembered for, I better start changing some habits in my life. This was a pivotal moment in my life. It was a true turning point. I hope you take this question seriously because it will change your life. I promise you.

For someone to understand himself or herself, they need to block the noise. I know partying and being social created a lot of noise and distractions in my life. Not that socializing is bad, but if you want to truly change your life, and start living meaningfully, this step is pivotal in doing so. I am not against drinking. I enjoy a few drinks. Some of my favorite moments in my life have happened while drinking. My favorite Christmas memory involves my Grandma and Grandpa and me over a bottle of Swedish Snaps, taking shots! It was great. But, the problem with drinking is that it can be abused. It can become a filter, a dam, or a roadblock that stops you from becoming who you really want to be. If you are not stable, drinking or other mind inducing substances can become your worst nightmare and lead you down a path that you did not know otherwise. Drinking can become a noise in your life.

The 90-day-sobriety challenge is what gave me the hope to see change in my life. How long is 90 days? 3 months? It is only a micro-portion of the entirety of your life.

The first week was the hardest for me. I wanted to drink so badly. The fact that I knew I could not drink, made me want to drink. People start looking at you different. At first, they wonder what is wrong with this guy, why doesn't he want to drink? But people will see your change and it will shed a light on them. You may not see it, but when they see your change, they will look deep into themselves and ask themselves who they are. It will be like them holding a mirror in front of their face, and it will hurt them. Most will flee with fear. However, the true warriors will hold fast and accept their flaws. They will begin to see a possible change in themselves. A change they might consider. Heck, if he can do it, why can't I? This logic will rise deep within their souls. If you have gotten this far in this book, it means you are different. The fact that you have invested in yourself to get to this page is a wakeup call. It is a pat yourself on the back moment. Go ahead, pat yourself on the left shoulder with your right hand! Good job! You are different! You hold unique gifts and talents that no one else has access to in this world besides you. AHH, what a beautiful thought. The thought of having access to only one key in the entire world, a key that can unlock the most precious jewels, a key that has more value than the rest of the world. It is so precious. Congrats!

Not drinking can become fun. Watching other people drink is sometimes more fun than drinking. It allows you to remain on top of yourself. It feels awesome being in control. People who drink more than they probably should lose themselves, they lose control. But that is why they drink that much, they want to lose themselves, they want to feel out of body. Just like Albert Einstein said:

"A person experiences life as something separated from the rest- a kind of delusion of

consciousness. Our task must be to free ourselves from this self-imposed prison, and though compassion, to find the reality of Oneness."

It is through drinking that people feel separated from the rest. It is where people find peace within themselves, *but it does not last, it only lasts a little while.* Take the 90-Day sobriety challenge and see yourself change. The best way to do this is to isolate yourself from the world, take the time to figure yourself out, and invest in yourself. Stop investing in other people, stop investing in socializing to fit in. You already fit in, you just have not realized it yet. I wish I would've known this in high school. It is something people sometimes learn in college, but even then, things never really change.

Attraction is not about sex. It is much larger than that. Attraction is about what you pull into your life! Now be careful, because the art of attraction can be abused if you are not stable as a person. If you do not know your intentions and if you have not answered *Question 1. "What you want to be remembered for after you die?"*, then you should not read this part. Attraction is a science, and successful people know these three things. They live by it. However, sometimes they use it for good and sometimes they use it for bad. I promise you, that if you use it for bad, it will hurt you.

Guaranteed. Here we go!

So, how do you become a more attractive person? Note, this applies to attracting humans, not just the opposite sex. Let me start of by telling you, attractiveness starts with relationships. As cliché as this may sound, it's true. We are surrounded by other people every day. People want to be happy, people want to be comforted, and people want to be loved by others. The point is, people want to feel appreciated and so do you, right? You can increase your attractiveness by implementing these three traits in your daily life:

1. How can I make other people feel appreciated?

Start by asking yourself how would I like to be treated? "Do to others as you would like them to do to you." Yes, this is true. Do this. Engrave this in your brain.

2. Talk less, listen more

People love to talk, and are very self-centered. Listening brings value into other people's lives. This can simply start by just asking a question.

3. Your Look (ex. clothes, hair, and hygiene)

Surely you have heard of the good old English idiom "don't judge a book by its cover." It is a metaphorical phrase which means "you shouldn't prejudge the worth or value of something by its outward appearance alone."

Well, it is bullshit, because people still make judgments. You don't have to be a vogue cover star to look good. You just need to tidy up. Show the world you care about how you look. By caring about how you look it will automatically increase your confidence. Confidence radiates attraction. Confidence is attractive.

The lack of honesty within ourselves kills who really are. Confidence is key to overcoming this. When you are confident, you are comfortable. When you are comfortable, you have peace of mind and your natural abilities and gifts have room to grow. If there is anything you should take out of this book it is confidence. It is an act of believing in yourself. Be confident. Be confident that you love yourself and do not let the opinions of others affect who you are. Confidence is what women are attracted to. Men think that attracts women, but it is really confidence that makes men attractive. Experience is everything. I can recall the times when I just sat, thinking, while anticipating acting. But fear somehow always gets in the way. There is nothing to fear. Truth be told, it seems to be a social norm to write about fear. The topic of fear is everywhere. Why do we fear so much? The famous line being, *what do we have to lose?* This question is one of the hardest questions in almost every person's life. We all face fear every day. Getting out of our comfort zone is not easy. It takes hard work, both mentally and physically. I don't know why I have feared so much. I know that most of the time there is nothing to fear and we are sometimes told to believe that there is nothing to fear. But truth is there is a lot to fear. However, fear is not the problem, it is your reaction to it. Embrace fear and react to it properly. Only you control and manage your fear.

Be honest with yourself. Lying to yourself can eat you alive. It has happened to me. The momentary pain will turn into a long unforeseen journey of pain. The pain that cannot be unlocked, but rather, it's aided by substances and short-lived band aids. Loving yourself begins with being honest with yourself. Confess you have problems, realize that you are not perfect, and that you are human and make mistakes just like everyone else. No one is perfect. Do not expect to be. Expect to be the best of yourself. Do not make excuses. Do not let the thoughts and opinions of other people hinder who you truly are and aspire to be. If you want to be in a play. Be in a play. If your friends do not support you, who cares? They will have to accept you for who you are no matter what. The fact is, people will grow with time. When you change it will take time for the people that love you to change as well. Think of it as a parallel growth between you and those in your life. It is time to let go of the negative thoughts. It is painful, but the future's so bright. You will grow into yourself. Be patient.

Cancelling the Noise

The funny thing about most people is that they are never truly comfortable with themselves. They go their entire lives finding comfort in all sorts of things. Things that do not make any sense, yet they still do it to feel comfortable. I am not perfect. I have so many flaws, but they are what make me who I am. It is what makes me different from other people, my imperfections are completely different than other people, no one else has the same exact flaws that I do. Maybe similar, but not exact. My flaws make me feel special. My imperfections are the very thing that lead me to my perfections.

Your imperfections are what make you beautiful. However, you will never understand this unless you isolate yourself from the rest of the world. You must cancel all the noise in your life in order to understand yourself. *When you understand yourself, then you can love yourself.* For example, you cannot easily love something you do not understand. People in relationships just don't love the other person without knowing who they are. Sometimes, people do love things they do not understand, and they end up getting hurt. I am going to give an example of what I mean by canceling all the noise in your life. Canceling the noise helps you understand yourself. Think of it as a bag and a vacuum. When you have a bag full of air, it is open to anything; dust and small particles can come in the bag. But when you vacuum seal that bag, you are left with nothing, just the bag. It is here that you will find yourself. With no air, no room to breathe, your natural state wants to breath, but in order to truly understand yourself you must be uncomfortable. When stripped away, you find yourself. During this uncomfortable time is when life begins, this is where your endless journey of joyful opportunities begins. Imperfections are the key to loving yourself. Stop filling the bag with air.

Get uncomfortable. Let go of your imperfections and embrace them. Most of us spend our lives on Facebook, Snapchat, Twitter, listening to music, and just absorbing too much noise. We are afraid of the silence. It is in the silence where you have your most intimate peace. The peace removes the clutter. The noise is just a distraction from the peace. Do not be distracted by the noise. Find that silence. Almost all of us are uncomfortable with silence, but loving yourself is uncomfortable, it is a relationship with your true self. It is only in your discomfort that you can find the comfort of your peace. Only in your imperfections, will you find your perfections. In the uncomfortable is your true self. *Now you can love others and their imperfections.*

A caterpillar and a butterfly are the same thing. Like a caterpillar I went into isolation. A caterpillar goes through metamorphosis, the stage in isolation before it grows it wings and reaches its full potential. In one month, I had gone from a totally broken soul to a person who was still broken. But I was a totally different broken person. I was a freed broken person and a loved person. Within 3 weeks of loving myself and taking the time to understand myself better I wrote this book and acted in 5 short movies.

The transformation of loving myself began to reflect positively on the people around me. My 12-year-old sister, Emma, started writing a book, *A Girls Guide to Middle School*. She has about 6,000 words so far. The book is going to be about how she experienced the reality of bullying in middle school. I am so proud of her! This is just one of the few amazing pieces from her book:

"One of my regrets of middle school is that I never put any interest in being in any clubs, sports, or group events. I was a wimp and I never put myself out there to find a good group of friends. Although I have good grades, I always took the easy way out. I never did anything extraordinary to make myself stand out as a

normal human being. And if you embarrass yourself, it's not as bad as you think because one day you'll look back and you'll crack the hell up."

My brother, Grant, has made the decision to move out and has taken the opportunity to move to Indiana. After attending a 2-week dive camp, he was recruited by a former US Olympic dive coach to come live and train in Indiana. By doing this, he is leaving high school early, at 17, and is going to live on his own in a totally new state to train 6 days a week doing flips and rotations off of a 10-meter-high dive and go to online high school and college. I am so proud! Both of my siblings have sacrificed, and it is so beautiful.

Loving Yourself

Love is an internal experience. Having peace in your heart starts by having a relationship with yourself. Loving yourself is oneness.

We must find truth within ourselves, no one else can tell you what truth is. You must believe truth yourself. As a young man that you are, you need to stand up and realize you will be faced with many roadblocks in your life.

Roadblocks are what make life interesting. Without the ups and downs, we do not fully understand what light and dark are. In order to experience happiness, we need to experience sadness. Henceforth, I am an advocate of the value of the energy of love and its divine power within us. It is what guides us in this journey of life to make it more meaningful.

A lifestyle without an eternal love sucks, because you are never truly satisfied. Einstein was right; without oneness, you will never be completely satisfied with anything in your life. You will always be searching for more, looking for better, and trying to get that next high. Your body is a temple. The world might not be, but your body is.

I will leave with you this; do not be self-destructive, do not hurt yourself.

Stop filling your life with the wrong things. It is time to fill your life with the right things. You are beautiful. You have goals. You have a direction and a vision. You know who you are and where you stand. You will not let anyone get in the way of your vision!

I want to thank you for reading. As, I sit here nearly finished writing it, I realize it has been a journey for me, not too long, and not too short, it has been just right for my first book. I encourage you to invest in yourself because you are the most important person in the world. This book was written in order to remind you that the internal prejudices in your life can dictate the course of your entire life and if you do not examine yourself, you might just regret it. Examining yourself is important because the only person that has control over you is you. I know this because my internal prejudices led me to a place I never want to go back to, and I have had to reexamine my life. Do not let the fear of falling keep you from flying. Only you control and manage your fear. YOU!

The best thing about loving yourself is that you can unlock the chains of fear. You are no longer tangled in the darkness of anguish and doubt. The view and sight of your future is unlocked. Love yourself! I believe the love within you will be one step towards a better world. Let love into your life. Let go and let love.

Made in USA - Kendallville, IN
1101621 9781688018037